Hidden in Plain Sight

A Guide to Unusual Public Art

Table of Contents

Chapter 1. Introduction

Step into a vibrant world of discovery and adventure that awaits just around the corner. Our special report, "Hidden in Plain Sight: A Guide to Unusual Public Art," uncovers the most extraordinary, yet lesser-known art installations scattered across parks, buildings, and sidewalks worldwide. Each page unfurls delightful surprises, revealing the creative brilliance hiding in our everyday landscapes. Profoundly captivating, this guide persuades you to see your environment through a unique, artistic lens. So, prepare your senses for a refreshing and thought-provoking journey. This report is the perfect companion for anyone looking to explore, appreciate, and celebrate the audacious genius of public art. Let's transform your ordinary walks into extraordinary art tours. Get your copy today!

Chapter 2. The Urban Canvas: Cityscapes Transformed

In the urban world, we often lose ourselves in the mechanical life devoid of modest beauty. Amidst the bustling streets and towering bricks-and-mortar buildings, a subtle artistic revolution exists, turning cities' blank canvases into living, breathing works of art. This cityscape transformation, spurred by countless creatives, injects life and color into our day-to-day environments, distorting our perspective on public spaces and evolving how we interact with the world surrounding us.

2.1. The Philosophy Behind the Mural

Murals constitute the cornerstone of urban canvas transformations. One must dissect the philosophy aimed to bind communities and uplift spirits through art. Diverging from sterile and often pressurizing gallery settings, artists discover cities' blank walls for their canvases, determined to express and provoke in the heart of society rather than its insulated corners. These art pieces intertwine with city life, irrespective of whether they're amidst the run-down buildings or shining on the chic streets of fashion districts.

The best part of contemporary murals is their inherent democracy. They are for the people, by the people, and of the people. Artists incorporate local culture, historical chronicles, and social issues in murals, entangling a piece of the community's soul with each brushstroke. Their work ignites dialogues, empowers marginalized voices, and allows art to step down from its elitist plateau to commune with the masses.

2.2. Cities as Artists' Canvases

Diving into art transformations of different metropolises around the globe, we find each city has its unique expression. For instance, New York City, birthplace of graffiti, has walls awash with strokes of subversion, portraying the rough yet resilient spirit of its denizens. In contrast, the street art in Berlin illustrates narratives of a tumultuous past, resilience, and unifying under a banner of freedom.

Paris, often celebrated for its pristine structures and high-end galleries, also hosts an array of public art transforming its traditional visage. The landscape pulsates with everchanging murals, including invader's street mosaics and Banksy's powerful commentaries plastered on the city's walls.

2.3. The Impression of Sculpture and Installations

Venturing beyond murals and graffiti, the urban transformation canopy extends to sculpture and installations, significantly impacting public spaces. These physical art expressions make viewers part of their narrative, inviting them to revolve and interact within a defined frame, breaking the barriers between observer and exhibit.

Chicago's Cloud Gate, colloquially known as The Bean, exemplifies how an installation can turn into a city's symbol. Its reflective surface plays with the cityscape around and the crowds approaching, providing a different perspective with every visit.

Less iconic yet deeply impactful is 'Fearless Girl' facing the Charging Bull on Wall Street. Initially installed as a temporary exhibit on International Women's Day in 2017, the statue garnered widespread recognition, becoming a symbol of gender equality and inspiring change beyond its immediate precinct.

2.4. The Role of Digital Projections

The dusk descends, and the cityscape dons a whole new attire. Digital projection art takes the center stage, lighting up buildings, bridges, and even water bodies. From using the ancient medium of shadow play to the latest lasers and drones, this evolving discipline is not merely painting the town with colors. It is changing the way we think about art, technology, and public space.

Highlighting Melbourne's 'White Night Festival', where the entire city transforms into a canvas for digital art, offers a panoramic view of this revolution. Iconic buildings and structures bear witness to narratives of culture, heritage, and discovery, told through interactive light projections, immersive installations, and music.

2.5. A Future of Evolution

As the world moves towards an uncertain future, the public art landscape finds itself standing at the crossroads of change. Climate-conscious creations are becoming the norm, with artists utilizing recycled materials and focusing on environmental themes. Digital interventions manifesting as augmented reality and virtual landscapes propose an unforeseen horizon of possibilities, spurring curiosity of where the transformation might lead us next.

Cityscapes have ceased to be mundane spaces. The cities, with their unexpected art outlets, are vibrant, living, breathing museums that are free and accessible. They stimulate, challenge, and inspire while also benefiting society's wellbeing, leading to a greater appreciation for contemporary art. However, the purpose of these transformations isn't just aesthetic. It is to create a dialogue, provoke thought, inspire change, and most importantly, make art accessible to all.

The urban canvas is far from complete, and its full potential is yet to be explored. Will our future cities be an intertwined collective of artists, community leaders, and citizens, creating together to make their surroundings a vibrant tapestry of narratives? Only time will tell.

Chapter 3. Nature's Galore: Artistic Brilliance in Parks and Gardens

Public parks and gardens serve as the lungs of our cities, and within these verdant spaces exist numerous treasures of public art hidden in plain sight. These underrated installations not only enhance the charm of these spaces but also narrate stories, provoke thoughts, and instigate conversations. Let's embark on this journey and bring these enigmas to well-deserved prominence.

3.1. Perspectives on Public Art in Parks and Gardens

Public art has a vital role in influencing the interaction between people and their environment, fostering connections that are both intangible and tangible. Art in parks and gardens often takes a backseat, mostly because of their unassuming and blended placement within nature, and the overshadowing influence of the natural beauty around them. But a closer look invariably reveals their significance, as we will explore in detail.

3.2. The Art and the Essence of Inclusion

One of the crucial roles that public art plays is that of inclusion. One can see this relationship mirrored in the works like 'The Awakening' - a 100-foot statue of a giant embedded in the earth, struggling to free itself. Installed in Hains Point Park, Washington DC, it has the power to transport the onlooker's mind into the mythical world, blending the ordinary with the extraordinary seamlessly.

On the other side of the world, in Sydney's Royal Botanic Garden, stands the 'A Folly for Mrs Macquarie,' an architectural work that serves as a place of rest and reflection. It captures the playfulness of a bygone era, thus giving past a tangible form in the present and inviting everyone to partake in that shared element of history.

3.3. Nature's Canvas: The Art of Landscaping

Landscaping in parks and gardens around the world holds a plethora of artworks to discover. These designs strike a delicate balance between being art themselves and offering a stage for other art pieces to flourish.

For instance, the 'Garden of Cosmic Speculation' in Scotland stretches the boundary of what is considered a combination of sculpture and painting on one hand and landscape design on the other. It comprises sharp, unconventional geometries, and mathematical and scientific concepts brought to life through undulating landforms and elaborately designed water bodies that bewilder and captivate the observer.

Meanwhile, New York's Central Park is a masterclass in balancing landscaping with sculptures and monuments. The intricately designed Bethesda Terrace features an iconic Angel of the Waters statue, marrying human artistry with natural beauty.

3.4. Stories in Stone: Monumental Art Installations

Monuments in public parks take many forms, from grand sculptures to mega-sized land art. 'Princess of Hope,' a natural rock formation in the Hingol National Park, Pakistan, intrigues visitors with its uncanny resemblance to a princess gazing into the distance. This naturally occurring sculpture elucidates how art can also be unintentional yet profound.

'El Drac,' or 'The Dragon' in Barcelona's Park Guell, is a tribute to Antoni Gaudi's genius. A vividly colored ceramic dragon greets visitors at the stairs, embodying the park's fairytale ambiance and Gaudi's organic architecture essence.

3.5. Conclusion: Reflecting on the Art around Us

Art found in parks and gardens is an essential facet of the public art domain. These spaces offer a creative experience that is free and accessible, blending creativity into our everyday landscapes in the most delightful fashion. More than mere decorations, these artistic pieces breathe new life into the parks, invite reflection, foster inclusivity, and narrate stories that are often overlooked.

Whether it is towering statues, architecturally intriguing follies, landscape designs pushing boundaries of creativity, or naturally occurring rock formations, these embodiments of public art demand a closer look, an acknowledgment of their existence, and a shared appreciation of their beauty and significance. They exemplify perfect symbiosis between human imagination and nature's generosity, transforming our ordinary walks into extraordinary journeys of discovery.

This exploration of art in parks and gardens worldwide is by no means exhaustive, as art is a dynamic, ever-evolving entity. But the intention is to evoke a sense of curiosity, encourage exploration, and heighten appreciation for these unique creations scattered around us, hidden in these lush landscapes in plain sight. Look around, and you may discover a masterpiece waiting to be admired.

Chapter 4. The Subway Series: Underground Art Installations

Public transportation becomes an everyday pattern for city-dwellers worldwide, involving strict schedules, repetitive routes, and familiar surroundings. However, those rush-hour rides can also take a delightfully unexpected turn when they intersect with art installations. Urban art, particularly within subways, transforms mundane commutes into a vibrant, creative expedition.

4.1. The Transformative Power of Art in Subways

With subway art, a commonly neglected corner of urban life turns into a realm of unexpected creativity and displays a city's cultural identity. These artistic installments are intentionally open to everybody, enabling maximum accessibility to art and making the city a grand, inclusive museum. They yield the powerful effect of injecting a certain charm in the daily rhythm of city-goers.

4.2. New York City: A Living Public Art Museum

Home to one of the world's oldest subway systems, New York City, unravels an immense tapestry of art in every corner of its underground network. Keith Godard's "Memories of 23rd Street," showcases life-size hats held by unseen personalities from the 1880s to the 1920s, reflecting the historical era. Another iconic piece is Roy Lichtenstein's "Times Square Mural" – an expansive mural in the Times Square station that portrays the future as the artist saw it in the comic-inspired style.

4.3. Stockholm: The World's Longest Art Gallery

The Stockholm metro system displays a unique combination of natural and man-made beauty. Often called 'the world's longest art gallery', over 90 of the 100 stations feature artwork - from mosaics to sculptures, paintings, and installations, each telling a portion of Sweden's history. Of particular note are Beda Hallberg's symbolic artwork in the Karlaplan station and the vivid nature-inspired paintings of Ulrik Samuelson in the Kungsträdgården station.

4.4. Naples: The Art Stations

In Naples, Italy, the subway transforms into a museum of postmodern art with its 'Art Stations' project. Artists, architects, and designers collaborated to create installations that blend seamlessly with the urban context, like the Toledo station's "Micro-organisms" mosaics by William Kentridge. The cosmic effects of the station, created by Robert Wilson's light panels and Oscar Tusquets Blanca's architectural design, leave commuters awestruck.

4.5. Moscow: A Tribute to Soviet Heritage

Moscow's metro system, known for its architectural grandeur, is also adorned with different art styles reflecting Russia's history. Soviet murals, stained glass depictions of historical events, bronze sculptures, and grand chandeliers hang in subway stations. The Komsomolskaya Station designed by Alexey Shchusev, featuring heroic murals painted by Pavel Korin, stands as the crown jewel.

4.6. Transforming Urban Landscapes

The thorough infusion of art within these subterranean transit spaces adds an aesthetic dimension to commuting, offering an escape from the mundane. London, Paris, Berlin, Seoul – cities globally are embracing art in public transit systems to improve urban spaces and provide cultural experiences to the masses.

4.7. The Impact on Community

Subway art installations have the potential to reflect diverse communities' experiences and narratives, fostering greater empathy and understanding among passengers. Beyond beautification, these vibrant additions serve as a reminder of the area's culture, history, and sense of place, enabling people to connect on a deeper level.

Today, experiencing art doesn't necessarily require a trip to the gallery. Instead, it can be enjoyed in the course up and down subway escalators, along platforms, or within the trains themselves. Public subway art changes the narrative of city transit, making it a treasure chest filled with cultural gems. Bright or somber, abstract or realistic, each piece of underground art has a story to tell. It captures the spirit of the city, highlights local heroes, challenges societal norms, and sparks discussions all while brightening up commuters' trips.

Interactive installations are also on the rise, turning passive observers into active participants. From magnetic poetry and mosaic puzzles to augmented reality (AR) experiences, this trend weaves the public into the art they encounter every day. A great example is the "Subway Therapy" initiative started by Matthew Chavez in New York City, consisting of sticky notes on the subway wall where passerbys were encouraged to express themselves post-election.

4.8. Future Perspectives

The resurgence of interest and investments in subway art points towards a brighter future for public art. Cities worldwide recognize the importance of integrating art into public spaces, especially in areas with enormous footfall like the subway systems. These installations dramatically alter the perception of these spaces, taking them from mere points of transport to sites of cultural interaction. Art in subways has the potential to be expanded and explored even further, thereby offering a continually evolving presentation of the city's heart and soul – displayed in its most hidden and yet accessible spaces.

4.9. Conclusion

From large-scale murals to intricate tile work, lights to interactive installations, subway art serves a dual purpose. It beautifies public spaces and underlines the intertwining of everyday life with culture, history, and the contemporary pulse. It encourages individuals and communities to observe, interpret, appreciate and partake in artistic dialogues, offering them a fresh perspective on their daily urban existence. Ultimately, subway art turns ordinary commute into a distinct experience of exploration - a journey through the conduit of a city's creative life-force.

Chapter 5. Resonating Echoes: Sound Art in Public Spaces

When one thinks of public art, the mind often conjures images of large-scale sculptures, grand murals painted on building walls, or eye-catching digital displays nestled within cityscapes. Despite this visual focus, there's an equally enthralling dimension of public art that frequently escapes the collective eye: sound art. This extraordinary art form makes a powerful impact on our perceptions and experiences of public spaces, offering a deeper, multi-sensory mode of engagement. From the delicate melodies of wind chimes to the rumblings of amplified geological shifts, Sound Art in public spaces presents us with an intriguing symphony of the world.

5.1. The Intricacies of Sound Art

Sound art sets itself apart from traditional art forms as it's primarily an auditory experience, attempting to create an immersive environment with the manipulation and orchestration of sounds. These are not random cacophonies but rather, a thoughtful, elegant harmony of ambient noises—nature's whispers, human-made tones, environmental echoes, conceptual frequencies—that engage a different sensibility in the observer or more aptly, the listener.

In many instances, sound art enhances the aesthetics of a public place and redefines how we perceive and resonate with our surroundings. Unlike visual arts, which often require a direct line of sight, sound art presents itself omnidirectionally and remains intangible, heightening our spatial awareness and creating an experience of place that is immersive, lively, and entirely unique.

5.2. Historically Speaking: Evolution of Sound Art

Sound art has been evolving for more than a century, marking a transformative journey from the avant-garde experimentation of Futurist Luigi Russolo's 'Intonarumori' in the 1910s, to the spatial installations of contemporary artists today. Early sound experiments, such as Russolo's noise-introducing orchestra, were brash, unconventional, and far ahead of their time.

In the mid-20th century, sound art underwent further evolution with artists beginning to interact with the environment and using recording technology. This novel approach led to genre-bending works like Max Neuhaus's 'Times Square', a sonic installation buried beneath a traffic island emitting resonating, melodic drone, almost surreal against the backdrop of Times Square's habitual clamor.

5.3. Soundscapes: Creating Auditory Landscapes

One critical element of sound art is the creation of 'soundscapes'. The term, coined by the Canadian composer and environmentalist R. Murray Schafer, covers an environment of sound (or sonic environment) with emphasis not just on the individual acoustic elements but on the way they interact and pattern themselves as a collective entity.

Artists create soundscapes in public places by intertwining natural and industrial sounds, setting up a thrilling composition that compels audiences to explore their environments more intimately. They envelop people in a sonic world, wherein each sound is as significant as a stroke of paint on a canvas—individual yet harmonious within the collective composition.

5.4. Amplifying the Geographical Features

Few artists navigate the path where they lay bare the sonic signatures of natural or urban structures, amplifying or adorning the sounds that already exist. Alvin Lucier's 'I Am Sitting in a Room' serves as a quintessential example. Lucier amplifies and re-amplifies his speech until the room's resonant frequencies fully consume the words. The muffled echoes that ultimately remain give life to the room's unique acoustics, capturing its unseen aesthetics.

5.5. Unseen Symphony: Sound Installations in Underground Spaces

Underground spaces possess unique acoustic properties, often existing as echo chambers for urban life above. Sound artists have long used these subterranean locales to create innovative installations. Bill Fontana's 'Harmonic Bridge' is one such piece, deploying acceleration sensors onto the structure of the Millennium Bridge in London to capture its vibrations and project them into Tate Modern's underground Tank rooms.

In conclusion, sound art offers a refreshing perspective on public art installations, underlining the significance of the unseen and the unheard within our everyday spaces. Despite its audaciousness, it plays along with the audience's curiosity, introducing them to the oft-overlooked symphony that exists in the mundane. As it evolves, this art form invites us to sharpen our senses, encouraging us to listen more closely and experience our surroundings more profoundly. By doing so, sound art transforms public spaces into resonating echoes of collective human experience, waiting to be discovered, celebrated, and understood.

Chapter 6. The Graffiti Paradox: Vandalism or Art?

Spray paint on a wall often presents a dichotomy of societal viewpoint: Vandalism or Art? It is within this binary, the story of graffiti unfolds.

6.1. From Ancient Doodles to Modern Murals

Roman walls bear testimony to the profound existence of graffiti, where it began as mere doodles or messages etched onto surfaces. Deciphered scribbles in Pompeii reveal advertisements for brothels, political rhetoric, and simple declarations of love. Travel further east, and Egypt's ancient monuments reveal detailed scribbles, incorporating the rich narratives of pharaohs and gods. From a historical perspective, graffiti has always been an inherent part of human communication strategy, a tool for masses to voice their opinions.

Fast-forwarding through millennia, our urban jungles have adopted graffiti as an indispensable part of the cityscape. Be it the vibrant color explosions on the New York subway trains in the late 70s or Banksy's provocative street art in present London streets, graffiti has formed a dialogue that transcends borders, age, and language.

6.2. Understanding Street Art and Graffiti

Before embarking on the journey of reading the metaphorical wall writings, it's important to understand the distinctions. Often blurring the lines, street art and graffiti are fundamentally different. Whereas graffiti emerged from a subculture, primarily focusing on scribbled, sprayed or scrawled stylistic alphabets - a tag representing the artist's pseudonym, street art pivoted towards a more illustrative and thematic approach. Akin to galleries exhibiting diverse artistic styles, from pop art inspired pieces, murals, stickers, to stencils - the streets began to speak in vibrant hues and narratives.

6.3. Graffiti: Vandalism or Art?

Herein lies the paradox - is Graffiti art? Or is it simply an act of vandalism? Intent and interpretation emerge as the quintessential factors to decipher this. If the intent is to merely damage property, with no artistic or symbolic value, it sways towards vandalism. However, if a piece is an endeavor to convey a message, challenge institutional norms, or simply exert creativity, it holds the essence of art.

Graffiti art, in essence, is a democratized form of artistic expression, mitigating the traditional barriers, to manifest itself in the public diaspora. It's important to note, though, what differentiates graffiti as art from vandalism is not just the aesthetic value but the intention to communicate and provoke thought.

6.4. The Legal Perspective

Legally, graffiti often falls under the disapproving tag of vandalism, primarily due to the unauthorized usage of public or private space. Laws vary widely, with some cities like Melbourne, Australia, adopting a more permissible stance, whereas places like Singapore mete out heavy fines for such activities. Conversely, famous graffiti locations like '5 pointz' in New York, 'East Side Gallery' in Berlin, serve as landmarks, attracting tourists, thereby contributing to the economy.

The complexity of the situation becomes evident when trying to categorize graffiti legally. While often considered illegal, it's important to note that some spaces do allow graffiti, therefore the art form itself is not illegal. Great debate surrounds this topic, and arguments from all viewpoints have been unable to reach a consensus.

6.5. Notable Graffiti Artists and Their Impact

There are several commendable artists who have used graffiti as a thought-evoking tool, lending it an air of legitimacy. Banksy, an anonymous England-based artist, is known for his satirical and subversive street art. His work comments on war, capitalism, and other social causes, poking holes in societal norms.

Jean-Michel Basquiat began as a graffiti artist in New York City in the late 1970s, under the pseudonym SAMO. His work brought contemporary African culture into conversation with the Western tradition, capturing the urban psyche and contradictions of his time.

Far from these hubs, in the favelas of Brazil, a duo known as Os Gemeos (translation: The Twins) provides a voice for the unheard, painting directly pertinent concerns and dreams.

These artists and others have steadily pushed graffiti away from Being regarded as mere vandalism, elevating it to a recognized, provocative form of public art.

6.6. The Graffiti Culture: Museums, Exhibitions, and Festivals

Conventional art spaces across the globe are opening their doors to graffiti exhibitions, recognizing and celebrating it. The Museum of the City of New York, for instance, had a grand exhibition titled "City as Canvas: Graffiti Art from the Martin Wong Collection". Such platforms bring together graffiti artists and enthusiasts, validating this art form and conferring upon it a sense of dignity and recognition.

Similarly, numerous graffiti festivals, like the Upfest in Bristol, UK, and the International Graffiti Festival 'Meeting of Styles', held across various cities worldwide, enhance the cultured status of graffiti.

No longer confined to the alleyways and dilapidated buildings, graffiti has transcended these boundaries and ventured into galleries and festivals, achieving the nod of the art world while continuing its foundation in dissent.

To conclude our exploration of this paradoxical art form, graffiti is not simply vandalism or art, but a combination, a reflection of societal conscience. Its public display steers our gaze towards the silent walls that hum with stories, beliefs, and the socio-cultural pulse of a city. And thus, while the debate continues, the spray cans rattle on; Graffiti, an unabashed, public voice inscribed on the canvas of the world. As reportage or defiance, cry of celebration, or anguish, it remains a fiercely indicting and intriguing element of our shared spaces. Naturally, the paradox persists, and so does the art form, connecting, communicating, and claiming its place in our daily lives.

Chapter 7. Architectural Alchemy: Building Facades as Art Pieces

Building facades have been subjected to artistic interpretation and experimentation for centuries, transforming them into ornate expressions of creativity and architectural prowess. These architectural marvels feature striking interplays of form, texture, and color, bridging historic practices with innovative techniques and materials.

7.1. The Harmony of Styles

The synthesis of classic and contemporary styles represents the essence of architectural alchemy. Although the origins of this intermingling lay in the Renaissance era, we are still seeing its evolution play out today.

Take, for example, the Louvre Pyramid in Paris, a masterpiece conceived by I.M. Pei. Amidst its historical surroundings, the pyramid brings a modern touch, blending steel and glass in a harmonious integration of old and new. A symbol of the fusion of styles, it embodies the transformative power of architectural design.

On another note, Gaudi's classical yet otherworldly Casa Batlló in Barcelona showcases a surrealistic façade, a realm away from his contemporaries. With its scales-like tiles and bone-shaped pillars, this building is an unmistakable work of art, standing as a testament to Gaudi's unique creative vision.

7.2. The Use of Innovative Materials

As architectural alchemy progresses, we're witnessing the ingenious use of innovative materials, defining the way we perceive and interact with building facaces.

The Mediacite shopping center in Liège, Belgium, is a perfect example of this transformation. Designed by Ron Arad Architects, its façade combines traditional brick with flexible, translucent materials, producing a captivating wave-like structure that attracts and fascinates.

Similarly, the MIKIMOTO Ginza building in Tokyo, Japan, an extensive use of steel and glass by Toyo Ito, creates visual complexity that defies uniformity. This masterpiece sets a new standard, challenging the traditional boundaries of architectural design.

7.3. The Intricacies of Structures

Innovative structural systems also play a crucial role in architectural alchemy. Traditional architectures are being pushed into the backdrop as new forms make their entrance, impressing viewers with unexpected geometry.

An exemplar of this is the Cube House in Rotterdam, Netherlands. Led by architect Piet Blom, this residential property challenges the typical face of buildings. Each house is designed as a tilted cube, resulting in altogether unique and imaginative spatial layouts.

Another extraordinary example is the Dancing House in Prague. A joint effort by architects Frank Gehry and Vlado Milunić, its non-rectilinear shape, inspired by dancers Fred Astaire and Ginger Rogers, adds a whimsical dimension to the city's otherwise traditional architectural landscape.

7.4. Public Sculptures on Facades

Public art has taken a central place not only as standalone installations but also as integral components of building facades — effectively turning walls into canvases for profound artistic expression.

A noteworthy example is the Empire State Building in New York. Not merely a skyscraper, it features a striking Art Deco style which celebrates modernity and progress, even as it remains a beloved skyline symbol almost a century after its creation.

Toronto's famous Gooderham Building, affectionately known as the 'Flatiron,' is another gem. Renowned Canadian artist Derek Besant transformed its rear façade into an optical illusion of a trompe-l'oeil, blurring the line between reality and visual interpretation.

7.5. The Impact of Light

Lighting technology has brought the ability to manipulate how we view architectural exteriors. From strategic spotlights to neon displays, architectural lighting can highlight design elements or completely transform facades after dark.

An exceptional example is the GLOW Eindhoven Festival in the Netherlands. This annual light art festival is dedicated to dynamic installations that revitalize architectural structures, immersing the urban environment in a fresh, illuminating perspective.

Crown Fountain in Chicago's Millennium Park is another example. A brainchild of Spanish artist Jaume Plensa, this installation uses light and water to breathe life into a foundational structure, serving as a beacon of creativity and innovation in urban design.

7.6. The Role of Technology

Technology plays a significant role in the evolution of building facades. From intensive 3D modeling in design phases to digital displays and augmented reality, the tools we have at our disposal are pushing the boundaries of possibilities.

The Future Systems's Selfridges Building in Birmingham, UK, stands as an excellent example of digital technology's impact on architectural design. The building's shiny, disc-covered exterior, conceived through complex computational design techniques, offers an immersive, textured gaze to passersby, turning architecture into a tangible art form.

In conclusion, the transformation of facades into art pieces is a testament to the ever-evolving relationships between form, function, and aesthetics in architecture. This shift is indefinitely making our cities and towns more visually engaging, a global gallery open for everyone to admire.

From the delicate merger of disparate architectural styles to the implementation of innovative materials and technologies, building facades are indeed an artistic playground that challenges our notion of the built environment. As we look ahead, it's exciting to imagine what other forms of architectural alchemy await us in the future. The perfect blend of art and architecture, these masterpieces offer us a fresh view of our urban landscapes, inspiring us to appreciate the beauty that's often hidden in plain sight.

As you explore these fantastic architectural artworks close up or even in your everyday encounters, let your senses explore, appreciate, and celebrate the architectural alchemy around you. Consider it a journey without an endpoint, an ongoing exploration of creativity placed boldly in the public eye. Who knows what magical transformations are yet to come.

Chapter 8. Pedestrian Rhapsody: Stories Told on Sidewalks

Sidewalks are perhaps the most utilized and yet underappreciated elements of public space. Mostly gray, often cracked, and commonly regarded as merely functional aspects of public infrastructure, these seemingly mundane paths are the freeways for pedestrians. And in their forgotten corners, brilliant artists leave their indelible marks, transforming the trodden paths into canvases that convey stories of humor, hope, and humanity. The following exploration uncovers pedestrian rhapsodies - stories told, quite literally, underfoot.

8.1. Graffiti Goes Legal: Rise of Sidewalk Chalk Art

In the 16th century, artists in Italy began transforming pavement into canvases using chalk, a tradition known as "madonnari" for their common depictions of the Virgin Mary. In the modern age, this practice has spread like wildfire across the globe. Visionary artists have emblazoned sidewalks with multifaceted imagery, from whimsical cartoons to stunning 3D illusions. This nouveau revival of chalk artistry has brought forth a new breed of talented creatives: the pavement Picasso, chalk Chagall, and crayon Kandinsky of the digital era.

Julian Beever, a noted artist in this genre, harnesses the principles of anamorphosis to create outstanding 3D masterpieces that coax one to question their perception of reality. These ephemeral chalk rhapsodies, though ephemeral, capture the public's imagination while they last, and inspire a fresh appetite for accessible street art worldwide.

8.2. Embedded Treasures: Toynbee Tiles

Sprinkled across the concrete jungles are cryptic messages known as the "Toynbee Tiles." Seemingly out of place, and yet so enigmatic, these intriguing installations have inculcated a sense of wonder and mystery in every passerby. The vividly colored linoleum tiles, primarily found in the Americas, bear variations of this cryptic message: "Toynbee Idea. Movie '2001. Resurrect Dead on Planet Jupiter." Their origin and purpose are unclear, with theories ranging from alien communication to a social experiment. While deciphering their meaning continues to mystify, their existence shakes up the mundanity of daily commutes.

8.3. Poesy of the Pavement: The Rainworks

Seattle, hailed for its high levels of precipitation and vibrant arts scene, is the birthplace of a unique form of public art called Rainworks. Invented by local artist Peregrine Church, Rainworks employs hydrophobic coatings to stencil artworks and messages onto concrete that become visible only when it rains. One may come across uplifting sentiments, playful graphics, or interactive games, transforming a drab, rainy day into an engaging experience. This distinctive blend of science and art demonstrates the boundless innovation possible in sidewalk artistry, making every wet walk an exciting treasure hunt.

8.4. Footprints in Time: Fossilized Art

In several cities worldwide, the past is embedded in the very sidewalks on which we tread daily. Literal relics of a bygone era, actual dinosaur footprints have been preserved in the pavement in localities like Morrison, Colorado. Elsewhere, artists take a more metaphorical route, incorporating motifs of fossils and ancient imprints into the sidewalks as seen in Roger Dean's neighborhood designs in the UK. These archeological art pieces prompt pedestrians to ponder over the relentless passage of time and the impermanent nature of existence.

8.5. Story Stones: Stolpersteine

Finally, lest we forget the darker corners of our shared history, artist Gunter Demnig began a poignant public art project known as "stumbling stones" or Stolpersteine. Across Europe, you may spot brass plaques nested amongst cobblestones that bear the names of Holocaust victims, marking traditionally the last freely chosen residences. The largest decentralized memorial in the world, these installations bid us pause and remember, humanizing the immense tragedy and making history tangible in our daily commutes.

The meandering pathways, stepped on by countless feet, are not just conduits for our daily lives but repositories of captivating art that offer a fresh perspective on our environments. They redefine our urban landscapes, compelling the pedestrian to look down not out of defeat but in joyful discovery of tales of persistence, creativity, history, and humor. These sidewalk rhapsodies encourage us to step outside the hustle, pause, perceive, and to connect with our cities on a more human level. Through their innovations, artists worldwide are turning these overlooked stages into public galleries, enriching our everyday with an imaginative ambiance, one footstep at a time.

Chapter 9. Artificial Arcadia: Virtual Public Art

Immersing oneself in the world of digital public art can transport you into an Artificial Arcadia—a realm where cutting-edge technology intertwines with artistic virtuosity. This form of public art has revolutionized the way we perceive, engage with, and experience art.

9.1. A Novel Realm: Exploring Virtual Public Art

Virtual Public Art (VPA) exists in a versatile space, unlimited by physical boundaries. Imagine art not restrained by galleries' walls or public parks' boundaries but resides in the virtual, expansive world—a fusion of reality and creativity maximized by the digital playground.

VPA can be augmented and virtual reality experiences, site-specific installations, online galleries, or even pixelated street art, confined not by geography but by the reach of technology. Massively multiplayer online games like Minecraft have given rise to intricate virtual sculptures and structures, proving the gaming world to be fertile ground for the imaginative artist.

9.2. From Cyberspace to Urban Space: The Manifestation of Virtual Public Art

A prime example of VPA transitioning from cyberspace to urban space is Pokemon Go. A seismic phenomenon upon its release in 2016, the game used Augmented Reality (AR) to populate real-world landmarks with virtual critters, turning city streets into an enormous digital artwork of Pokemon habitats. Pokestops and gyms, digitally plastered onto landmarks, had players returning to the same public spots, mirroring a pilgrimage to a favorite art installation.

Bloomberg Connects' digital engagement program offers another innovative blend of technology and engagement with art. With its tailor-made app, visitors can delve into stories behind the art pieces, participate in artist-led activities, and share their experiences on a digital guestbook.

9.3. The Democratization of Art Through Technology

In VPA, accessibility and inclusivity are taken to unprecedented levels. Unlike traditional public art, which is occasionally unreachable due for various reasons, VPA has the potential to reach billions worldwide with internet access.

Online galleries are prime examples. Google's Arts & Culture platform made it possible to tour the likes of the British Museum or the Van Gogh Museum without leaving your home, ensuring that cultural treasures are not limited to in-person visitors alone. Simultaneously, the platform allows artists worldwide an undeniable chance to showcase their talents to a broader audience, inspiring artistic creation and appreciation alike.

9.4. Contemplating the Virtual: The Aesthetics and Philosophy

Nevertheless, the virtual realm challenges our traditional concepts of aesthetics and art. If it exists only in pixels and cannot be touched or materially experienced, can it be art? The answer seems to lie in philosophical interpretation. Aristotle's theory "Art = imitation of life" validates virtual art's existence. VPA imitates or appropriates physical reality, yet adds new dimensions to it: interactivity, hyperrealism, or even dystopian versions of 'what could be'.

We stand on this digital threshold, peering into a virtually infinite realm rich with potential. AR, VR, online galleries, and gamified street art are but embryonic stages of virtual public art, yet their impacts on aesthetics, engagement, philosophy, and accessibility are profound.

9.5. Future Impressions: VPA Post-Pandemic

The COVID-19 pandemic has further propelled VPA. With public spaces locked down, artists have sought novel ways to engage audiences, and virtual realms provide a perfect playground.

Public artworks have begun to inhabit digital spaces more prominently. Music concerts, previously confined to stadiums and concert halls, are now being staged on Fortnite, a videogame platform, transforming these virtual arenas into stages for musical expression.

Artists and institutions, too, are increasingly exploring NFT (non-fungible token) art. This innovation allows artists to create unique or limited-edition digital works, enabling art ownership within the virtual space.

9.6. Conclusion: Embracing the Virtual Paradigm

In conclusion, Virtual public art is an expansive, immersive domain of infinite possibilities. As digital tools and technology evolve, public art will continue to transgress boundaries, leaving us in anticipation of what our pleasant strolls in the virtual park will discover next.

In this era of digital renaissance, our job as observers, participants, or creators is to keep our senses curious, stay open to changing notions of public art, and witness the blossoming future of virtual public spaces. This world of Artificial Arcadia is truly a limitless canvas, and the brush strokes have only just begun.

Chapter 10. Candid Moments: Unintended Art in Everyday Life

Art is often an organized and considered act, a deliberate creation where each stroke or word is chosen with care. Yet, just as often, art is something more elusive and unpremeditated, the result of our daily hustle and bustle — the unintended art in everyday life. In busy streets, playgrounds, or shopping centers, art emerges in the most unsuspecting moments and places. This chapter serves as an ode to these candid masterpieces — simple, unendingly diverse, and wholly ingrained in our lives.

10.1. The Suspended Poetry of Clotheslines

For many, clotheslines are merely functional, a medium for drying wet clothes. However, when viewed through the lens of involuntary art, they reveal layered narratives and subtle beauty. Stroll through any residential neighborhood, and you'll see a collage of clothing swaying in the wind — a vibrant artwork splashed against the blue canvas of the sky.

Garments in every size, color, and design drape off lines, weaving tales of the families they belong to. A red dress may stand out against a field of white shirts, implying a spark of individuality in an otherwise uniform existence. A row of children's clothing may symbolize the predominance of youth and energy. Clotheslines, when viewed as a spontaneous urban installation, inspire us to look beyond the mundane and appreciate the art woven within our daily routines.

10.2. Tumbling Treasures: Graffiti and Street Art

Graffiti has long held an ambiguous position between vandalism and art. This expressive form, once considered a visual blight, now commands a unique aesthetic status. Its spontaneity and impermanence echo the transience of urban life.

Exploring the city, one will encounter an eclectic mix of simple tags, elaborate murals, and thought-provoking pieces of social commentary. The brick walls of old buildings become the canvases for artists' expressions. Undulating lines, vibrant colors, and cryptic messages reflect the echo of a cultural dialogue — alluding to the zeitgeist in a way that formal galleries often fail to capture. This ever-evolving art form quashes the boundaries of traditional art, urging us to question the conferred importance of permanence in defining artistic worth.

10.3. Unscripted Drama: Shapeshifting Shadows

Sunlight and shadows have conspired to render the world their canvas since time immemorial. However, their ephemeral performances often escape our notice — fleeting and unpredictable. A mural stretching across a winding sidewalk, vanishes under the cloak of clouds. Building facades bathe in soft, golden hues during sunset, only to yield to an inky silhouette with twilight.

Shadows shift, conveying an evolution of meaning – a boy reaching out to a branch transforms into a mythic giant; a tree oscillates between ominous and majestic depending on the sun's arc.

The drama of light and shadow yields a different masterpiece each day, inviting us to appreciate the fleeting beauty they encapsulate and our environment's continually changing aesthetics.

10.4. Sidewalk Superheroes: Chalk Art on Concrete Canvases

Sidewalk chalk art is a magical medium that transforms concrete into colourful playgrounds. Its inherent transiency adds a certain poignancy to the spectacle — a light drizzle or a busy footpath could erase these ephemeral masterpieces.

Chalk art festivals worldwide celebrate this form of public art, showcasing intricate murals that might trick your imagination with their meticulous 3D illusions. However, it's not just the grandiose creations that deserve a second glance. A child's naive sketch of their family or a whimsical doodle on a deserted alleyway packs as much emotion and wonder. These slices of unplanned creativity serve as heartwarming reminders of children's boundless imagination and the inherent human impulse for artistic expression.

Each day, life presents us with an ever-revolving gallery of involuntary art. These offerings are everywhere, hiding in urban landscapes and waiting for us to shift our gaze and appreciate the art embedded in our existence. By acknowledging them, we weave ourselves into a larger tapestry — a living artwork home to a billion candid moments. Welcome to the gallery of life.

Chapter 11. Vision for Tomorrow: Evolution of Public Art

In the beginning, public art was a means for society to express cultural identity and communal values. Stonehenge, the Sphinx, Mayan ruins - these early examples still resonate with their audiences thousands of years later. Respected, appreciated, and often mystifying, their presence in the public domain was intended. These ancient pieces of public art served a spiritual and functional purpose, creating spaces for community gatherings and celebrations, weaving narratives of a culture's history and mythology, and fostering a collective sense of identity.

11.1. From Monuments to Modernism

From these early monoliths, public art began to evolve. Consider how statuary developed in Ancient Greece and Rome, examples of which are extant today and continue attracting tourists worldwide. Statues were meant to immortalize heroes, gods, and significant historical figures, concretizing societal values in bronze or marble.

This tradition carried through the Middle Ages and into the Renaissance, then further refined during the Enlightenment. Statues, murals, and architectural embellishments spoke volumes about a society's identity and aspirations, effectively marrying artistry and influence.

With the advent of the Industrial Age and the influx of new materials and techniques, public art began to push boundaries and reimagine itself. The onset of Modernism saw public art move away from conventional forms, such as statuary and monuments, towards abstract and conceptual expressions.

11.2. The Rise of Interactive and Inclusive Forms

The 20th century brought forth a democratization of public art. While monuments and great works were niche and often government commissioned, this new wave of public art was accessible, engaging, and populist in nature. Artists sought to actively involve the public, transforming art from a passive spectacle into an active engagement, pushing the viewers to become co-creators and interpreters of the artwork.

Public art installations began to value diversity, interactivity, and inclusivity. For instance, graffiti — once considered an act of rebellion and vandalism — became a legitimate, revered form of public art. It amplified voices from segmented and marginalized communities, providing a platform for discourse, protest, and expression.

Temporary art exhibitions and installations also surfaced, offering a dynamic, ever-changing landscape. These exhibits, like the renowned Burning Man Festival or the temporal art installations in Montreal's Quartier des Spectacles, are platforms for artistic exploration and public participation.

11.3. Into the Digital Age

Today, public art has transcended the physical world, permeating into the digital realm. Virtual and augmented reality technologies have broadened the horizon of what public art can achieve. Artists can now construct intricate, immersive worlds, transcending the constraints of physical space. Digital domain artworks are accessible anywhere, anytime, removing geographical restrictions and increasing the artwork's reach.

As we gaze into the future, it becomes evident that the evolution of public art aligns with societal changes, reflecting contemporary discussions and global narratives. In an age of increased digitization and technological advancement, art is no different. It promises exciting possibilities, such as art installations powered by artificial intelligence or projects exploring the intersection of human consciousness and virtual reality.

11.4. Sustainability and Public Art

The importance of sustainability in every aspect of our society has led artists to integrate this concept into their work. Materials used in public art are being reconsidered with a focus on using recycled, biodegradable, and environmentally friendly alternatives. Cities across the globe are transforming with 'green art' — artworks and installations that raise awareness about environmental issues or contribute positively to the environment.

A compelling example of such sustainable public art includes wind sculptures, utilizing natural elements as a part of the art. In some cases, public art has even been used to generate renewable energy, showcasing the symbiosis between artistic expression and ecological responsibility.

11.5. A Platform for Social Commentary and Change

Despite the changes in form and medium, the core of public art remains a platform for expression and communication. Artists are leveraging public art as a mode to highlight pressing social issues, propel cultural conversations, and ignite change. It remains a potent tool to promote unity, diversity, and social justice, contributing significantly to community growth and transformation.

To conclude, the evolution of public art is reflective of our society, a mirror to our innovations, aspirations, and challenges. With increasing recognition of its potential, public art continues to evolve, augmenting our public spaces and enriching our shared experiences. Tomorrow's public art looks set to be a vibrant fusion of technology, interaction, sustainability, and social commentary, promising profound and inspiring future encounters.